Cornerstones of Freedom

The Story of

Yellowstone National Park

Deborah Kent

CP CHILDRENS PRESS®

CHICAGO

Library of Congress Cataloging-in-Publication Data

Kent, Deborah.
  Yellowstone National Park / by Deborah Kent.
    p. cm. — (Cornerstones of freedom)
  ISBN 0-516-06678-1
  1. Yellowstone National Park —Juvenile literature.
[1. Yellowstone National Park 2. National parks and
reserves.] I. Title. II. Series.
F722.K4 1992   93-37521
978.7'52–dc20   CIP
                                          AC

"Standing there . . . I thought how utterly impossible it would be to describe to another the sensations inspired by such a presence," wrote explorer Nathaniel P. Langford in 1870. "As I took in this scene, I realized my own littleness, my helplessness, my dread exposure to destruction, my inability to comprehend the mighty architecture of nature." Langford wrote these awestruck words from a height overlooking the Midway Geyser Basin on the Firehole River. For hours he and his companions gazed in wonder as boiling water erupted from the depths of the earth. The geysers created a fantastic, ever-shifting panorama—plumes, cones, and fan-shaped towers of steam.

Midway Geyser Basin—a wondrous sight to 1800s explorers

Early explorers were awed by Yellowstone's strange natural formations.

Reports of mysterious wonders in the northern Rocky Mountains first reached the settled parts of the United States in 1807, when explorer John Colter described hot springs bubbling with brimstone, or sulfur, along the Gardner River in present-day Montana. Colter seemed to be a reliable witness. Four years earlier, he had traveled west with the Lewis and Clark Expedition to explore some of America's newly acquired western territory. But his latest stories were so bizarre that few people believed him.

Through the decades that followed, Americans pushed westward with the ax and the plow, turning forests and prairies into farmland. In 1848, gold seekers rushed to California, and white settlements spread along the Pacific Coast. Yet the upper Rocky Mountains remained almost untouched by white people. One area within this region was known to the Dakota Indians as *Mitsia-Da-Zi*, or "river of the yellow rocks." From these Indian words comes the English name that has been used for more than a century— Yellowstone.

Trappers and prospectors brought months of supplies as they ventured into the mysterious western regions of North America.

The vivid colors of Yellowstone's thermal waters are caused by algae, bacteria, and other tiny organisms that thrive at high temperatures.

Jay Cooke

Over the years, the Yellowstone region gave rise to a series of strange and improbable tales. Trappers and prospectors claimed to have seen seething pools of rainbow-colored mud, trees boiled to death by steam, and a forest turned to stone. Most people dismissed these reports as the ravings of men who had spent too much time alone in the wilderness.

In 1870, Jay Cooke of the powerful Northern Pacific Railroad Company hired Captain Henry D. Washburn, an experienced surveyor, to lead an expedition into the fabled Yellowstone country. If the amazing stories had any basis in fact, the Northern Pacific might someday bring trainloads of tourists to view the natural wonders.

The Washburn party quickly discovered that the stories were true indeed. The Yellowstone region was a stunning landscape of geysers and thermal pools, petrified forests and cliffs of glass. It was a vast terrain of unrivaled mystery and beauty, a land unlike any the men had ever seen.

Visitors are still amazed by the dramatically different kinds of terrain found at Yellowstone.

While camping beside the Firehole River (right), the Washburn party decided that the Yellowstone region must be preserved for posterity.

One evening, three weeks after Langford first saw Midway Geyser Basin, several members of the expedition sat around a campfire at the fork of the Firehole and Gibbon rivers. As they marveled over the wonders they had seen, a daring new idea was born. To this day, no one knows who voiced it first. But suddenly, the men around the fire knew that the Yellowstone region must never be mined for gold or cleared for cultivation. It must be preserved intact for future generations. Later that night, one of the explorers, Cornelius Hedges, wrote in his diary, "God made this region for all the people and all the world to see and enjoy forever. . . . Let us make a public park of it and set it aside, never to be changed, but to be kept sacred always."

After the expedition, Washburn, Langford, and the others toured the nation, giving public lectures about the extraordinary places they had seen. Within months, Ferdinand V. Hayden, director of the U.S. Geological Survey, led a team of scientists into the Yellowstone wilderness. While botanists, zoologists, and geologists studied the natural history of the region, artists and photographers created a dazzling record of the landscape in pictures.

Ferdinand Hayden

Artist Thomas Moran was brought on the Hayden expedition to make a visual record of the Yellowstone region. The Grand Canyon of the Yellowstone (left) is one of many paintings Moran developed from his sketches after he returned home from the trip.

As soon as he returned to civilization, Hayden teamed up with Langford, Washburn, and the growing crowd of scientists who hoped to preserve Yellowstone for posterity. As they lobbied Congress, they had the backing of Jay Cooke and the Northern Pacific. Cooke was convinced that a public park in the Yellowstone region would be a boon to the railroad industry, and he wielded tremendous power in Washington, D.C. He was a man accustomed to getting his way—and this was no exception. On March 1, 1872, President Ulysses S. Grant signed the Yellowstone Park Act, creating the first national park on earth. The act stated that

Aspens at Yellowstone in autumn

Yellowstone National Park embraces a wide range of environments, including grassy plains dappled with wildflowers.

Yellowstone should be a "pleasuring-ground for the benefit and enjoyment of the people."

Carved from territory that later became the states of Wyoming, Montana, and Idaho, Yellowstone National Park sprawls over 2.2 million acres. The park is roughly square-shaped, measuring about 55 miles on each side. The largest wildlife preserve in the United States, Yellowstone embraces a wide range of environments, from wetlands and grassy plains to stately old-growth forests of lodgepole pine. Much of the park is a high, wind-swept plateau that rises

Steam erupts from Castle Geyser.

some 3,500 feet above the surrounding terrain.

The Yellowstone region rests on one of the world's "hot spots," a place where molten rock, or magma, from the earth's core bubbles toward the surface. The immense pressure of this magma forces the earth's crust to bulge upward, forming the plateau that can be seen today. Around the base and sides of the plateau, the earth is riddled with cracks. Groundwater seeps through these cracks to the magma chamber below, is heated to boiling, and bursts to the surface again in the form of geysers.

In 1872, when Yellowstone was declared a national park, the only Indians who lived there permanently were a mixed group of Shoshone and Bannock Indians known as the Sheepeaters. Their name came from their staple diet, bighorn sheep. Most whites believed that Indians avoided the Yellowstone region because of superstitions about its geysers. Archaeologists, however, have found that hunters and gathers roamed the area since the end of the last Ice Age, about 11,000 years ago. Some 250 Indian sites have been discovered in and around the park. Stone from Yellowstone's Obsidian Cliff, prized for making axes and other tools, has been unearthed as far away as present-day Illinois.

A glacial boulder in the Lamar Valley of northeastern Yellowstone

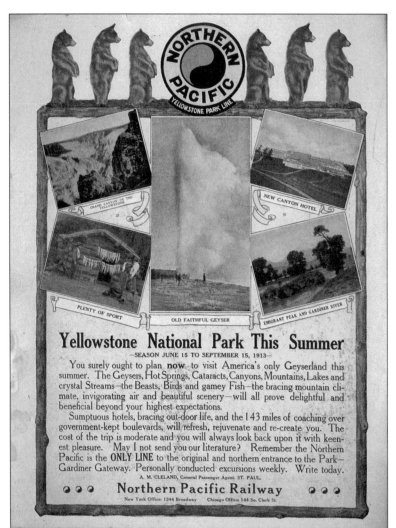

In the late 1800s, the Northern Pacific Railroad started an advertising campaign to draw tourists to Yellowstone.

At first, Congress allotted little money for staff and maintenance at Yellowstone. Lured by the Northern Pacific's advertising campaign, tourists fished the streams with abandon, slaughtered elk, bears, and mule deer, and painted their names on rare rock formations. Some discovered that they could trigger especially violent eruptions by dumping soap into the geysers.

Clearly, something had to be done, or the beauty of the park would be lost. In 1886,

Congress put the management of Yellowstone into the hands of the United States Army. From a fort near Mammoth Hot Springs at the park's northern rim, soldiers fanned out through the forests in search of poachers. They launched special efforts to protect the park's bison, the last remnants of the vast herds that once roved the Great Plains. In its eagerness to protect elk, deer, moose, and other game animals, the army declared war on natural predators. Relentlessly it hunted and poisoned wolves, coyotes, and cougars. The military also established a strict fire-prevention policy. All forest fires in the park were hastily extinguished, whether they were caused by lightning or human carelessness.

In 1902, President Theodore Roosevelt paid a visit to Yellowstone. An ardent big-game hunter

Tourists at the park in the early 1900s

U.S. Army officers patrolling the park in the late 1800s

Teddy Roosevelt

and amateur naturalist, Roosevelt thrilled to everything he saw. "During the two hours following my entry into the park, we saw probably a thousand antelopes," he wrote later. "One morning, after a careful count with binoculars, we reckoned three thousand head of elk, all in sight at the same time. . . . Surely our people do not understand even yet the rich heritage that is theirs."

Most early visitors to Yellowstone were wealthy vacationers who belonged to the upper echelons of society. The Northern Pacific delivered them to Cinnabar Station near the park's northern entrance. From there, regular stagecoach service set them down at their first stop, Mammoth Hot Springs. Generally, visitors opted for the "Grand Tour," a five-day stagecoach journey that covered the park's most famous sights. The tourists gazed in wonder at Obsidian Cliff, where Indians once gathered stone for making weapons; the

Tourists pose in front of Rainbow Geyser in 1919.

More than a century after the park's founding, visitors still love to tour the Mud Volcano (left) and observe wild elk (above).

Fountain Paint Pots, hot pools tinted by pink, orange, green, and yellow algae; and the Mud Volcano, a seething cauldron of gray mud where the ground trembled underfoot and the rotten-egg smell of sulfur hung in the air. They admired herds of grazing elk and threw scraps of food to black bears that begged beside the roads. They rode by steamboat over the icy waters of Yellowstone Lake, or explored the Grand Canyon of the Yellowstone River on horseback. "The

Steep, jagged cliffs and a silky white waterfall make the Grand Canyon of the Yellowstone one of the area's most stunning sights.

Grand Canyon of the Yellowstone is the most sublime sight I have ever seen," one young man wrote to his family. "We rode on narrow, steep bridle paths, part of the time through pines, part on the edge of cliffs way above the Yellowstone River. . . . At Lookout Point we seemed to be up in the air, and up the valley saw the Lower Falls, over twice as high as Niagara."

Throughout the park, visitors saw erupting geysers. Although Old Faithful was not the biggest—Grand Geyser spouted twice as high—it quickly became a cherished landmark. At predictable intervals of thirty to ninety minutes, Old Faithful sent spires of scalding water 100 to 140 feet into the sky. In 1904, park concessioners opened the magnificent Old Faithful Inn, overlooking the geyser. Thought to be the largest log structure in the world, the inn featured a vast, balconied lobby—open to the roof eighty-five feet above—with all its rustic wooden beams and braces exposed to view.

Left: Old Faithful, one of Yellowstone's most famous attractions
Right: The magnificent wood-beamed lobby of the Old Faithful Inn

Each year, more and more people venture into the remote areas of the park to hike and camp.

In 1916, the federal government created the National Park Service, an agency within the U.S. Department of the Interior. Headed by Stephen T. Mather, the Park Service was given full responsibility for Yellowstone, as well as for California's Yosemite, Washington's Mount Rainier, and several other parks that had been established in the preceding decades. At Yellowstone, park rangers replaced cavalry troops, and a new era began.

The coming of the automobile brought the park within reach of thousands of families who could not afford the old-fashioned Grand Tour. After 1915, when cars were first permitted in the park, the number of visitors redoubled with each summer season. The park saw a brief lull during World War II, but tourism soared in the post-war years. In 1948 the park received 1 million visitors; the yearly number reached 2 million in 1966. Over the years, more and more people left the popular sightseeing areas and ventured into the remote backcountry to hike and camp.

Fishing at Yellowstone

Yellowstone was created as a "pleasuring-ground for the people." It was meant to be used and enjoyed. But how could elk, bison, bears, and other animals survive amid hordes of

Balancing the needs of Yellowstone's human visitors with those of its animal inhabitants has been an ongoing challenge for park officials.

Some of the park's residents: Elk (left) and a moose (right)

camera-snapping humans? Scientists, congressmen, and Park Service officials debated the question endlessly, but no one had an answer. As the world's first and busiest national park, Yellowstone was a bold experiment.

The elk population was a troubling example of the problems confronting park authorities. After the army and the park rangers wiped out wolves, cougars, and other predators, the number of elk increased dramatically. Eventually, the elk exhausted their food supply. In the harsh winter of 1919-20, thousands of these majestic animals starved to death. Yellowstone superintendent Horace M. Albright began to feed the wintering herds with bales of hay, but the problem did not go away. Elk devoured everything within their reach. They started land erosion by consuming grasses and underbrush, and killed trees by stripping off their bark.

In the 1950s, the park began a new policy. It halted winter feedings and shipped as many elk as possible to zoos and to other parks. But even these measures were not enough to keep the population within bounds. In 1961, "direct reduction teams" of park rangers shot 4,300 elk inside the park. In the early 1970s, elk were driven from the park to be killed by hunters waiting just outside its limits.

When President Grant signed the Yellowstone Park Act in 1872, scientists knew almost nothing about ecosystems—the interaction among flora and fauna in a given area. The army and park rangers tried to protect the so-called "good" animals such as elk and bison by killing off the "bad" wolves and cougars. This human interference caused a monumental shift in the natural balance among Yellowstone's creatures and the plant life they needed for their survival.

A bison and its calf

In the early 1960s, Yellowstone officials initiated a plan to restore the park as nearly as possible to its original condition. Botanists replanted prairie grasses that had nearly died out over the past century. Biologists reintroduced wolves and cougars. Park rangers closed garbage dumps where black bears and grizzlies had fed for generations. This, the rangers hoped, would force the bears to return to a more natural

The park's "let-it-burn" policy is based on the idea that natural fires actually help keep forests healthy by destroying old, dead timber and fertilizing the soil with ash.

existence in the backcountry. There was even a new attitude toward forest fires. Fires that occurred naturally, by lightning, would be allowed to burn unless they endangered human life or property. Scientists were realizing that fire plays a vital role in keeping forests healthy— opening meadows among densely packed trees, and fertilizing the soil with ash.

The park's "back to nature" policy delighted most environmentalists, but it was not easy to carry out. Wolves and cougars were unimpressed by boundaries on a map. Wandering out of the park, they outraged neighboring ranchers by attacking sheep and cattle. Bears, too, became a menace when deprived of the garbage that had long been their food supply. After the dumps closed in 1968, hungry bears began to forage around campsites. Several campers were injured, and a few were even killed.

At first, the new forest-fire policy had little impact on the park. Each summer, lightning started dozens of blazes that burned out quickly, leaving few marks on the landscape. When the first natural brushfires flared in 1988, no one suspected trouble.

The summer of 1988 was the driest in the park's recorded history. Dead leaves and branches covered the forest floor like a carpet of kindling. As the summer passed, brushfires swirled higher, climbing the trunks of mighty trees. The wind picked up flaming twigs and pine needles, and flung them down to spark fresh fires miles away. By the end of July, flames engulfed 16,000 acres

During the unusually dry summer of 1988, brushfires at Yellowstone—which normally burn out by themselves— turned into major blazes. Firefighters were called in, but the situation was beyond human control.

Spectators watch as the fires of 1988 rage on.

Firefighters get ready to help in September 1988

of parkland. Yellowstone officials decided that the natural burning had gone far enough.

Nearly 10,000 firefighters poured into the park, while others battled blazes in the national forests nearby. But eight major fires raged on. On September 7, a biologist named Steve French wrote from Antelope Valley, "Fire absolutely everywhere—up to the ridge, all through the upper meadows and interspersed trees. The meadows were circled in fire rings. Trees were exploding, crashing, echoing constantly. I can't imagine anything surviving it. It pains me to think of hundred-year-old whitebark pine stands being evaporated in less than a minute." Ultimately, it was the change of season—the snowfall and cold nights that began on September 10—that finally brought the fires under control.

The fires left more than one-third of the park in charred ruins. Many anguished citizens blamed park officials, claiming that the park's natural-burn policy was ill-conceived. "The ground is sterilized," Senator Alan Simpson of Wyoming declared before Congress. "It is blackened to the very depths of any root system within it." Many experts, however, insisted that no amount of human intervention could have stopped the blazes. As one veteran firefighter from the area pointed out, the park had so many acres of old brush and old timber that, when

Cold weather and snowfall finally put out the flames.

A thermal pool in the aftermath of the 1988 fires

combined with such dry conditions, "Yellowstone was a ticking time bomb."

Despite the devastation, the following spring, larkspur, Idaho fescue, and a host of other wildflowers burst through the scorched soil into rollicking life. Tiny seedlings poked through the blanket of ash, the fragile beginning of a new forest. As many environmentalists had predicted, Yellowstone was beginning its long, slow cycle again, a natural cycle of destruction and renewal.

Fire is not the only threat facing Yellowstone in the years to come. Growing crowds flock to the park each year. In winter, snowmobiles tear up

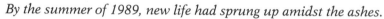

By the summer of 1989, new life had sprung up amidst the ashes.

Visitors attend an outdoor class on Yellowstone's thermal features.

the ground; in summer, backpackers disturb shy, nesting songbirds. The habitat is shrinking for elk, grizzlies, and other large mammals whose natural territory extends beyond the park boundaries. In the national forests surrounding the park, developers harvest timber and mine for gold and other minerals. The 1990s saw plans to exploit the region's geothermal energy—the power that fuels Yellowstone's geyser basins. Some scientists warn that excessive drilling could destroy Old Faithful and other Yellowstone geysers, and might even trigger earthquakes and volcanic eruptions.

In an effort to preserve the remaining wild lands in and around the park, more than thirty-five organizations joined forces to create the

Greater Yellowstone Coalition in 1983.
Yellowstone itself is only a fraction of the vast
region of mountains, lakes and forests in the
upper Rockies, an area that spreads over some
18 million acres. The coalition works to balance
the interests of developers with the needs of the
region's inhabitants—both animal and human.

Today, streams of automobiles rather than
stagecoach caravans follow Yellowstone's Grand
Loop Road. Many still enter the park at
Mammoth Hot Springs, where water cascades
down a series of limestone terraces that gleam
turquoise, coral, and gold in the sunlight. Old
Faithful still performs on schedule, and the Old
Faithful Inn stands in the forest like a cathedral
hewn of logs. In the Hayden Valley, bison, elk,
and mule deer graze calmly along the road. There
are still boat trips across the blue, icy waters of

*Minerva
Terrace at
Mammoth Hot
Springs*

Yellowstone Lake, and hikes or horseback rides along the Grand Canyon of the Yellowstone River.

Despite the crowds, the paved roads, and the skeleton trees left by the 1988 fires, Yellowstone still offers the unique vision that stunned the early explorers. The words conservationist John Muir wrote in 1885 are just as true today: "A thousand Yellowstone wonders are calling. Look up and down and around about you . . . and learn that here is heaven and the dwellingplace of the angels."

INDEX

PHOTO CREDITS

Picture Identifications:
Cover: Moonrise at Old Faithful
Page 1: Lupines in a meadow at Yellowstone
Page 2: Grand Prismatic Spring, near the Firehole River

Project Editor: Shari Joffe
Designer: Karen Yops
Photo Researcher: Jan Izzo
Cornerstones of Freedom Logo: David Cunningham

ABOUT THE AUTHOR

Deborah Kent grew up in Little Falls, New Jersey, and received her B.A. from Oberlin College. She earned a master's degree in social work from Smith College, and worked for four years at the University Settlement House on New York's Lower East Side.

Ms. Kent left social work to begin a career in writing. She published her first novel, *Belonging*, while living in San Miguel de Allende, Mexico. She has written a dozen novels for young adults, as well as numerous nonfiction titles for children. She lives in Chicago with her husband and their daughter Janna.